Mopeding

CHARLES COOMBS

Mopeding

illustrated with photographs

William Morrow and Company   New York   1978

Library of Congress Cataloging in Publication Data
Coombs, Charles Ira (date) Mopeding.
   Summary: Discusses the purchase, maintenance, and use of vehicles that are driven either by pedals or motor. 1. Mopeds—Juvenile literature. [1. Mopeds]   I. Title.
                         TL443.C67   629.22′72   78-18394
            ISBN 0-688-22155-6   ISBN 0-688-32155-0 lib. bdg.

Printed in the United States of America.
First Edition
1   2   3   4   5   6   7   8   9   10

All photographs are by the author with the exception of the following: Batavus U.S.A., page 120; byKart, Inc., page 112; Italjet U.S.A., page 118; Malaguti of America, page 23; Minarelli U.S.A., page 42; Motobecane America, Ltd., pages 33, 43, 53, 110, 116; Motorized Bicycle Association, pages 16, 33, 66, 80; Paul Soni of America, Inc., page 19. Permission is gratefully acknowledged.

For William Campbell Gault,
friend and fellow writer.

Contents

Foreword

It is always pleasant and exciting to tackle a book on a subject that is fairly new and growing rapidly. Certainly mopeds fall into this category. They are not entirely new, however, for motorized bicycles of one kind or another have been found in the United States for years.

But now they are around in the hundreds of thousands, and soon perhaps in the millions. Mopeds are handy, practical, safe, economical, and fun. I speak with at least a little authority, since I myself own and use one.

But more than personal experience is needed to write a book about mopeds. I had to do a great deal of studying, talking to manufacturers and dealers, testing of machines, and corresponding with authorities. In general, I had to master the subject of mopeds and mopeding.

No matter where I went, or with whom I talked,

there was boundless enthusiasm for these machines. This made the research and picture gathering very enjoyable.

I hesitate trying to single out those who were most helpful. Everyone associated with the companies and agencies listed under the photograph credits, and some not listed, were fully cooperative.

However, a few deserve special mention. For instance, through the courtesy of Dolph Varner and Jeff O'Reilly of American Garelli, a trailer load of mopeds was delivered to me. For a month the entire neighborhood had fun riding them. It was interesting to see how quickly people of all sizes and ages, unfamiliar with motorized two-wheelers, adapted to the small, low-slung, stable mopeds.

Helen Schwartz, of Motobecane America, also extended extraordinary help. M. Paul Zimmerman, Executive Director of the Motorized Bicycle Association, was quick to supply important information and materials. Mrs. Mildred Palmer, of Palmer Industries, provided a most worthy treatise on the subject of electric-powered mopeds.

And my thanks to Charlie Kaljian, coproprietor of our largest local moped center, who furnished many good pointers and checked out the final manuscript.

12

Add, of course, the two fine young people, Janet and Tom Roche, who appear in many of the photographs. Neither had ridden a moped before, yet by the end of a full, busy day both were delighted "veterans." We got our pictures, and everyone had fun.

In fact, I suppose if there is any single key word to mopeding, that is it—*fun*.

To all the helpful people, named or unnamed here, my sincere thanks.

Charles "Chick" Coombs
Westlake Village, California 1978

1 The Versatile Moped

Take "mo" as in motor, add "ped" as in pedal, and you have "moped." But what is it? What you have is a small, lightweight machine that is a cross between a motorcycle and a bicycle. You may be tempted to call it a motorized bicycle, which in most cases it is not. Or you may think of it as an underpowered motorcycle with pedals added, which is not completely true either. A moped is a moped—a handy two- sometimes three-wheeled vehicle with its own design and its own purpose.

A moped is relatively inexpensive to buy. It is simple to operate, cheap to maintain, decently quiet, and easy to park. In addition, it is quite safe when properly ridden. Mopeds consume small amounts of fuel, and they don't pollute, at least not noticeably.

Thus, a moped seems to meet the need of getting around without using an expensive, smoking, gas-guzzling, four-wheeled vehicle. In many respects it is

a dream machine compared to the noisy, high-powered motorcycles that dodge dangerously over the highways or go spinning and churning over sometimes fragile terrain.

Students, commuters, fathers, mothers, sons and daughters, vacationers, farmers, sportsmen—anyone

16

looking for handy, inexpensive, uncomplicated, short-range transportation is a potential mopeder.

Mopeds and mopeding on a large scale are quite recent developments in the United States. However, the manufacture and use of motor-assisted bicycles has been common for several decades in other parts of the world.

By the end of World War II, petroleum products, particularly gasoline, were both scarce and high-priced in many areas outside the United States. Bicycles had long been a common means of transportation in Europe, Asia, South America, and in most distant lands. Pedal power was the propellant used by millions of people to get around.

Following the War, as cities expanded and spread out, more and more people migrated to outlying areas. Distances from schools, work, and recreational activity increased dramatically. Unassisted pedaling often became more of a chore than a healthy pastime. So ingenious cyclists began experimenting, by attaching small motors to their bicycles, to ease the burden of pedaling.

Although the word *moped* is believed to have originated in England, the manufacture of bicycles with booster motors on a commercial scale probably began on the mainland of Europe, perhaps France. Most were gasoline powered. A few were electric. Many were ordinary bicycles with power units attached to the front or rear wheels. Once the pedaler got the vehicle moving, the small auxiliary unit was started up. Riders could then simply rest their feet on the pedals and enjoy the trip. If they encountered a hill or bucked into a stiff head wind, they renewed pedaling in order to assist the straining, low-powered engine.

At first simple motor-assisted bicycles, moped machines have changed and improved dramatically during recent years. But their primary function remains unchanged—to make short-range transportation economical, less strenuous, and more pleasant.

Narrow streets, scarcity of parking space, high cost of gasoline, traffic congestion in the cities, plus a minimum of restrictive rules and regulations combined to popularize mopeding in many foreign countries. Then, when the energy crisis occurred in the mid-seventies, the boom in mopeds spread to the United States. Today there are probably more than fifteen million mopeds on the streets of Europe and more than half a million in the United States. Worldwide estimates vary from forty to fifty million mopeds, put-putting in cities and across countrysides, from Acapulco to Zanzibar.

Most mopeds are manufactured in foreign lands.

Most of the mopeds found throughout the world are made in Europe. France, Italy, Austria, Germany, Holland, Sweden, and Czechoslovakia account for a major number of today's mopeds. Japan and Taiwan are moving strongly into the field too. Now several manufacturers in the United States are also producing

American "bikes," as mopeds along with bicycles and motorcycles are commonly called. The three-wheeled mopeds are logically called "trikes."

A moped fits a variety of descriptions. It might be gasoline-powered or battery-powered. Its motor may be mounted over the front wheel, near the rear wheel, or in between. It may be chain-driven, belt-driven, or propelled by friction rollers rubbing directly against the wheel to turn it. It can resemble a bicycle, but rarely does. Yet it is usually legally classified as a bicycle rather than a motorcycle. Thereby the owners may avoid having to register and license it. Riders need not carry insurance or wear a helmet. A few states do not require a mopeder to have an operator's license.

The latter point should be carefully noted. A moped is designed primarily for use on public streets and country roads. And, despite the small size of its engine, its limited speed, or its similarity to a bicycle, a moped is a motorized vehicle. In many states only a person possessing a valid driver's license can operate one. Even when a license may not be required, there is often a minimum-age limit for riding a motorized bike on a public thoroughfare, generally within the range of fourteen to sixteen years old.

Like dirt-bike motorcyclists, mopeders can also enjoy off-road activity in certain permitted areas. It is not possible, however, to duplicate the feats of the motorcycle hill climber, the motocross expert, or the cross-country racer. Except on decently packed paths and fairly level trails, the low-powered moped simply is not a dirt machine.

In appearance, mopeds more closely resemble lightweight motorcycles than they do bicycles. Yet the handlebars, hand-brake levers, and foot pedals are similar to those on a bicycle. The combination of a small motor and pedals are what distinguish a moped from any other transportation vehicle.

Despite similarities, differences, or legal classifications, you should think of your moped more in terms of a motorcycle than a bicycle. The machine is engineered more for using motor power than pedal power. It is too heavy a vehicle and its chain geared too low to pedal any more than is absolutely necessary. Ninety-nine percent of the time you will probably rely on power from the small engine. And when you ride a powered machine of any type you must abide by the laws and regulations that govern any other motor-driven vehicle, whether it be an automobile, a motorcycle, a motor scooter, or whatever. You can no longer ride in the casual, often careless, curb-jumping manner of some bicyclists.

So, first and foremost, a moped is a machine. Further, it is a relatively simple machine that is low-powered and fairly slow moving. It varies in size, color, and design. Yet, despite slight differences in design and manufacture, most mopeds seen around the world fit into one basic, easy-to-recognize pattern.

The typical moped is built on a frame that is considerably heavier and stronger than that of a bicycle. The frame is usually a step-through type, only slightly reminiscent of the frame of a girl's bicycle. The open frame enables you to get on or off without having to swing a leg up over a high horizontal, bicycle-type crossbar or over a gas tank, as is characteristic of motorcycles.

A moped gas tank is usually a small slanting receptacle fastened on the forward tubing of the frame. Near the base of the frame, below the gas tank, the engine is mounted. It is a small one-cylinder, two-stroke type, a cousin to those used on power lawn mowers, chain saws, and small outboard motorboats.

The legal size and power of the engine varies from state to state, although efforts are being made to establish national standards for moped engines. In order to

The moped has a distinctive low-slung, step-through frame.

keep the moped well out of the category of motorcycles, the size of the motor must not exceed fifty
cubic centimeters (50cc) of cylinder capacity. The
motor also is limited to two horsepower (hp) or less.
Depending upon the gearing and ignition system, this
tiny air-cooled engine can accelerate the moped to

maximum speeds of twenty, twenty-five, or thirty miles per hour, according to whatever speed restrictions are established by local laws.

Sticking out from each side of the machine, near the motor and transmission assembly, are the pedals. They are linked to the motorized sprocket, thus enabling the rider to use leg power to propel the machine without the engine or to help out when the small motor begins to labor.

The most familiar moped wheel is a much-strengthened version of a bicycle wheel. Although smaller in diameter than many bicycle wheels, measuring generally around sixteen or seventeen inches, the wheel is beefed up with heavier spokes and a strong, wide rim that takes two- to two-and-a-half-inch broad-treaded, high-grade tires. Some bikes have wide mag wheels, with several heavy, nonadjustable, pressed spokes supporting the rim.

Since a moped weighs around 100 pounds, two or three times that of a bicycle, it needs good brakes. The rim-squeezing caliper brakes found on bicycles will not do the job. So the average moped of good quality has internal-expansion drum brakes on both front and rear wheels. You operate both brakes by hand levers similar to those on many bicycles and thus

24

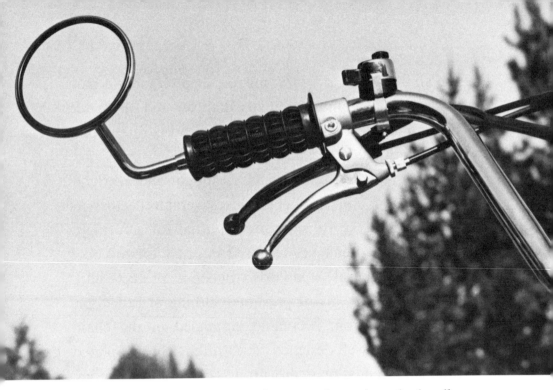

Switches, control levers, and mirrors are located on the handle-bars.

eliminate the foot pedal used for the rear brake on motorcycles. These small drum brakes are highly effective and meet strict Federal safety standards. The brakes must have inspection windows through which you can check the condition of the brake lining inside the drum.

Additional attachments are also needed for a safe and comfortable ride. Mounted on the handlebars are assorted switches, brake levers, a horn button, and

25

the all-important rearview mirror, or preferably a pair of mirrors. A combination speedometer and odometer is mounted near the handlebar post and is often combined with the head lamp.

A high-quality, sealed-beam headlight and a bright-red taillight and stoplight, plus several reflectors at the rear and on the sides are essential for safe night riding. These items are required in order for the bike to meet Federal standards. Fenders protect both wheels. A chain guard prevents clothing or other foreign objects from becoming entangled in the chain or belt. A well-designed and often chrome-plated muffler extends rearward from the motor, carrying away the hot exhaust gases and reducing the bark of the two-stroke engine to a reasonable purr.

Add a comfortable, adjustable, spring-supported padded seat, a handy carrier rack behind it, a center-mounted kickstand for upright support, and your typical moped is complete.

There are, of course, many other items that you can add to your bike. Some are more decorative than func-

a deluxe moped with turn signals and windscreen

tional. Do not, however, weigh down your vehicle with unnecessary accessories. Keep it as lightweight and maneuverable as possible. Also the lighter the weight the better mileage you will get. One of the moped's most appealing qualities is that of needing little gasoline. Depending upon the machine, the type of terrain being ridden over, and the load being carried, the average moped will get from 100 to 150 miles on a gallon of gasoline.

So, if the extent of your traveling will be too much for a bicycle, if a motorcycle is too expensive to buy and maintain, or if you are looking for a recreational vehicle that you can help pedal up a hill when you want exercise, the power-assisted moped may be what you need. A moped is not all things to all people. It has both good and bad points. Only you, through inquiring around, checking out machines, and taking a few demonstration rides, can determine which moped, if any, fulfills your transportation requirements. Only you can decide whether or not mopeding is for you.

But it can safely be said—and you need only look around you for ready proof—the moped has definitely arrived.

2 Choose the Right Machine

Searching for the proper moped to fit your particular needs can be complex. There are more than two dozen brands and usually several different models of each. And there are widely assorted dealers all trying to promote and sell their particular machines. Unless you know at least fairly well what you are looking for, the whole process can be puzzling.

First you should consider how you intend to use your moped, if and when you get it. If you want to take long-distance cross-country trips, climb steep mountain trails, or do acrobatics, a low-speed, low-powered moped probably is not for you. But if you are looking for a mechanically simple, easy-to-operate, inexpensive-to-maintain utility machine, exploring available mopeds can be a rewarding experience.

A moped is not a mere toy. It is a legal transportation vehicle subject to Federal, state, and local laws governing the ownership and use of all roadworthy machines. Study these rules and regulations before you buy. Check with your Department of Motor Vehicles, which should be well informed on the subject. Inquire at the city hall in your area for any additional rules that may affect the operation of your moped.

Remember always that your moped will face the dangers of the road as well as the pleasures. It will be only as safe as you make it by properly maintaining and operating it.

There are numerous places, including some dealers,

a moped dealer

where you can rent a machine. After you have tried out several mopeds, you might find it wise to rent your favorite bike for an hour or so and give it a good trial run before you purchase. Some dealers, after having judged you a serious and capable rider, will allow you a free test. Whatever the arrangement, at least get a good preliminary idea of what you are looking for. Find out whether or not mopeding is what you expected it to be. Chances are you will be delighted.

You might even consider shopping around for a secondhand moped. You could find a bargain, or you could end up with a lemon. Always check out a secondhand machine more thoroughly than you would a new one. After all, the used bike carries no manufacturer's warranty, and, unless it is purchased from a reputable dealer who stands behind his product, the risk is all yours.

Assuming, however, that you've decided to shop for a new moped, what's the best way to do so? Since a new moped generally will cost somewhere between $300 and $600, depending on the make and model, there is a built-in incentive to look around before deciding. Consider first the dealer. Mopeds are featured and sold by an increasing number of dealers who sell and service the machines. In addition, bicycle shops and motorcycle agencies often handle mopeds as a second line. Some brands of mopeds are featured in automobile showrooms or automotive-supply stores. You might also find mopeds on sale in hardware stores, discount houses, department stores, or even in some drugstores.

Wherever your search takes you, one of your first considerations should be whether the sales agency carries spare parts and offers reliable service. It is frustrating to purchase a moped and then not be able to find a replacement part or a trained mechanic who can fix it, if something goes wrong. Since mopeds are fairly sensitive machines, it is important that you can contact someone who is sufficiently trained and skilled to keep your bike finely tuned.

Most, but certainly not all, mopeds are collections of foreign-made parts—for instance, the frame from Taiwan, motor from Italy, wheels from France, shocks from Germany. If you buy an Austrian Puch, a Dutch Batavus, an Italian Garelli, a French Motobecane, an American Columbia Commuter, or any other brand, first be sure that parts are available and service facilities are included in the package.

Many moped manufacturers, both at home and abroad, have had valuable prior experience in build-

Training schools prepare moped dealers and mechanics.

ing motorcycles—Indian, Motobecane, Garelli, Puch, Honda, and Peugeot, to name a few. This experience does not, of course, guarantee top quality, but it is something to consider. Plenty of fine machines are built by bicycle manufacturers or by companies that turn out mopeds exclusively.

33

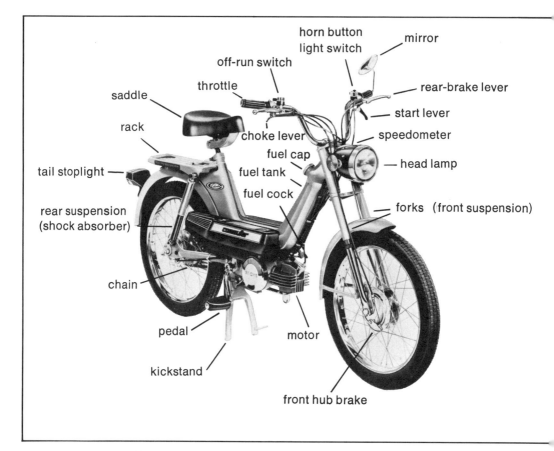

the basic parts of a moped

Usually it is cheaper in the long run to shop for quality. An extra fifty or a hundred dollars in the purchase price may pay off handsomely later on in fewer faulty or worn-out parts and less emergency service and maintenance.

While shopping around, sit on a lot of machines. Find one that feels comfortable and solid. The more

34

low-slung the moped is the better it will hug the road, and the more stable it is apt to be. A long wheelbase, or distance between the front and rear hubs, also helps provide firm steering control and adds riding comfort. When you find a bike that is comfortably stylish and pleases you, give it a good going over.

Check the frame for cracked paint around the welded joints. Whether it is a tubular frame or one made of pressed steel, go over it carefully, particularly at bends and around stress points. Check anything that is attached to the frame and make certain it is properly welded or firmly bolted. Do the same with any of the fiber-glass moped bodies and parts now on the market. In all cases be sure the wedding of parts is smooth and solid.

Inspect the gas tank. Is it of sufficient size to provide an ample riding distance—say, up to a hundred miles—between gas stops? Generally that will mean a capacity of approximately one gallon. Is the tank solid and thick-walled so it will resist rupture? Is it firmly attached to the frame and located where it is least vulnerable to damage in case of a fall or an accident? Does it have a leakproof cap that won't jar loose unexpectedly?

The tank is usually mounted on the forward rise

of the frame. Indeed, at times it is part of the frame, molded into it during manufacture. Some mopeds have high horizontal tanks similar to motorcycles. Consider the tank carefully. As the container of volatile fuel, any failure on its part creates an immediate hazard.

A good suspension system is extremely important for comfortable, safe riding. Most all quality mopeds have both front and rear shock absorbers. The front shocks form the wheel forks. The rear pair of shocks serve to soften the bumps that would otherwise pass directly from the back wheel to the frame. Telescoping, oil-loaded hydraulic shocks are usually considered preferable to the coiled-spring variety. Yet either, if properly adjusted, effectively helps smooth out road bumps. Often there will be coil-spring shocks on the front wheel and heavy-duty hydraulic shocks on the rear wheel.

Since contact with road or path is made through the wheels and tires, be sure to get the best quality. Raise the bike onto its centered kickstand, and spin each wheel in turn. Sight along the rim to detect any warp or wobble. Plink the wire spokes, keeping your ears tuned to changes in sound that indicate loose or overtightened spokes. A pleasant musical ping indicates proper tension. If the bike happens to have mag wheels, with heavy, built-in spokes, you need not concern yourself with problems of tension.

Don't compromise on tires. Be sure they are of top quality. Reputable tire companies such as Pirelli,

Good-quality tires are essential.

Michelin, Semperit, Continental, and others fabricate tires just for mopeds. There are both tube and tubeless tires. They are properly reinforced to handle the substantial weight of moped and rider safely. Their treads are designed to maintain the best possible traction on dirt, sand, or pavement, wet or dry.

If a tire carries the letters DOT on the sidewall, it means that the United States Department of Transportation has approved the tire and that it meets Federal specifications on mopeds. The tire also should have the size, types and number of plies, proper inflation figures (twenty-five to thirty-five pounds per square inch, psi,), safe speed (normally not over thirty miles per hour), and load maximums (around 180 pounds), stamped on the side.

While you're looking over the wheels and tires, give more than a passing glance at the brakes located in each wheel hub. The drums should be sufficient in diameter and width to accommodate good-sized, internal brake shoes. Usually the bigger they are the better the braking surfaces. Make sure there are built-in inspection windows, as required by Federal

Large brake drums indicate adequate brake shoes and good stopping ability.

standards. They make it easy to check periodically on whether the brake linings are getting worn.

Inspect the brake cables leading to both front and rear hubs. Are they firm and neatly laid out? They must be looped enough so there are no kinks or binding corners to restrict the movement of the cable inside the housing. But the loops and twists should not be so big that they vibrate or whip in the wind.

Despite the fact that the drum brakes themselves are similar to those on motorcycles, the hand-control levers are modeled after the caliper brakes on lightweight bicycles. The levers should be strong and firmly anchored to the handlebars. And, of course, they must be within convenient reach of your handgrips.

Turn your attention now to the cantaloupe-sized motor mounted low under the forefront of the frame. Consider it closely, for it is the power plant that may someday carry you over hill and dale, to school, to the store or the pizza parlor. As it goes, so go you.

Some of the most reliable names on moped motors are Sachs, Puch, Morini, Peugeot, Garelli, Laura, Honda, and Minarelli. Some others, less known, are equally efficient. Testing will tell the story.

At least 90 percent of the time, the motor will be a

the motor

single-cylinder, two-stroke, air-cooled gasoline engine, which generates somewhere between 1 hp and 2 hp. The closer you get to the maximum legal moped power of 2.0 hp and a full 50cc of allowable cylinder space, the better off you probably are. At best, that's

41

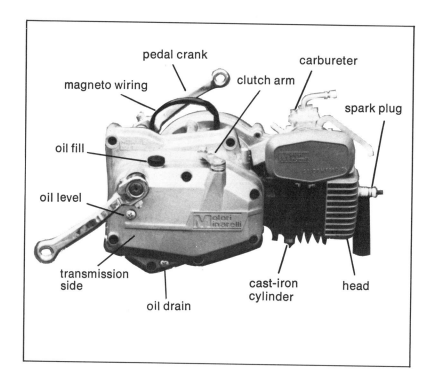

pedal crank

magneto wiring

clutch arm

carbureter

spark plug

oil fill

oil level

transmission side

oil drain

cast-iron cylinder

head

a low enough power boost for a vehicle that may weigh up to 300 pounds, including machine and rider.

The higher the motor's power rating, the better your throttle response will be and your ability to accelerate when necessary. Also the more power you have, the less motor strain there will be during normal or uphill riding. You may get fewer miles per gallon (mpg's) with the larger engine, but they still will probably exceed a hundred, no matter what type of engine you choose.

Check on the cylinder head to be sure there is

adequate cooling surface. Raised fins absorb and help dissipate the heat built up inside the motor.

Make sure that the spark plug is easy to reach, for you will want to be able to remove it easily and clean or replace it at regular intervals. Also, are the carburetor and air filter handy for cleaning and servicing? Accessibility to parts is important on mopeds, because there are many cleaning and minor servicing chores that you may want to do yourself in order to cut down on maintenance costs.

A two-stroke engine is a model of simplicity. The air-fuel mixture from the carburetor is drawn into the crankcase on the upstroke of a tiny piston. As the spark plug ignites the earlier charge, driving the piston back downward, the fresh mixture in the crankcase is forced through a transfer port, a tunnel of sorts, up into the combustion chamber. At the same time, spent gases exit from the combustion chamber through an exhaust port.

The two-stroke engine is so named because the piston moves up (one stroke) and down (the second stroke) with each firing of the spark plug. The piston is coupled by a connecting rod to the crankshaft. As the piston shuttles up and down inside of the cylinder —perhaps at 4000 to 5000 revolutions per minute (rpm)—it spins the crankshaft. A transmission, or centrifugal clutch, transfers this crankshaft power to running a chain or belt that turns the moped's drive wheel. This so-called power train does not require a hand-operated gearshift or other manual control, since the transmission, or clutch mechanism, works automatically. Moped transmissions are either dry-friction types or an oil-bath (wet) variety not unlike the automatic transmission of an automobile. Some wet transmissions have variable-ratio drives that automatically adjust the gearing to suit the power demands of climbing a hill or cruising along a straightaway. Many of the better bikes also have automatic, two-speed transmissions.

One of the distinguishing features of a moped is that at times of overloading, if the engine begins to balk, you can use the helper pedals to support the power system.

The two-stroke engine is nicely suited to mopeding. It has no valves, so there is no problem of burned-out valves or periodic valve-grinding jobs. Given reasonable care, it will propel you many thousands of carefree miles between major overhauls. Belts and chains are easy to adjust and care for, and the entire power train operates freely and without complication.

44

bench, or buddy seat, for extra comfort

Power for spark-plug ignition, as well as for the headlight, taillight, and stoplight, is usually provided by a small flywheel magneto, which is part of the motor and transmission assembly. You will want to be sure that the magneto puts out enough power to operate all electrical systems on your moped. Usually your lights will work properly only when the machine is running under normal throttle. They will dim somewhat when you cut the throttle to idle. Some mopeds, however, have a small battery of reserve power for use when the machine is not operating. This reserve is used particularly for operating turn-signal lights, optional equipment on most mopeds. Whatever type of system you have, don't underestimate the importance of a reliable electrical supply for your moped.

In the interests of comfort, consider carefully the seat, or saddle. Be sure it is well-padded and spring-mounted. You may prefer the bench, or buddy-seat, style, although you should be wary of carrying passengers on your moped. It is normally not safe and often not legal.

While shopping for your moped, consider fenders and carrying rack behind the seat. Fenders are quite necessary on both front and rear wheels if you hope to stay at all clean while traveling. Most fenders are painted to match the frame. But some quality bikes have fenders made of molded plastic, bright stainless steel, or chrome. The main consideration is that the fenders provide proper protection.

If the moped has a carrying rack mounted over the rear wheel, it may also have a rattrap spring to hold down books or small packages. If the rack is not sufficient for your anticipated loads, you can buy auxiliary baskets or saddlebags for added carrying capacity. Bicyclelike handlebar baskets are available but less favored than rear-mounted baskets. Loading up the front end of your moped makes steering more difficult.

speedometer-odometer

Most mopeds have a strong, center-mounted, folding kickstand. When the bike is parked, the stand balances it with its rear wheel off the ground. This center stand keeps the moped much more firmly upright than does the single, side-hinged bicycle kickstand.

Another part to consider when inspecting the moped is the muffler, which should be solidly mounted and sufficiently packed and baffled to reduce engine noise as much as possible.

Then, too, you will need certain accessories. An important one is a combination speedometer-odometer to tell how fast you are going and how far you have gone. Laws in some states require a speedometer. Most states also require you to have some kind of a rearview mirror mounted on your handlebars. Flat rather than rounded mirrors are recommended. The latter do afford a wide-angle view of things to the rear, but the distortion makes everything appear so far back that you cannot judge distance accurately. Two mirrors, one on each tip of your handlebars, are better than one and help to erase potential blind spots behind you.

While shopping around, you might consider adding leg shields to your moped or a plastic windscreen, or both. Check with your dealer to see if these items are available, just in case.

Have fun when you are picking the color of your moped. Bright crayon colors predominate, and wisely so, for they add to the visibility of your machine. That in itself is a safety factor. You can even arrange for hand-painted striping if you wish.

Once you are well into the search, and after you have talked with a lot of people, looked at and tested a number of mopeds, the picture of what you really want will begin to form clearly in your mind. Finally, you find a machine that strikes your fancy. It appears to be sturdy and reliable. Its lines are graceful; its paint is pretty. It carries a label issued by the Motorized Bicycle Association (MBA), attesting to the fact that it meets established Federal standards.

All in all, you think you have found the moped you are looking for. Now you want to make sure. The time has come to check it out thoroughly, so get ready to fire it up and take it on a trial run.

3 The Trial Run

Before you go tooling around on a moped, ask yourself this question: Am I moped-riding material? If you can ride a bicycle, any bicycle, probably you are. In fact, you will find that a moped, with its stabilizing, low center of gravity, automatic transmission, and few controls to operate, is considerably easier to ride than a ten-speed bicycle. The main difference is that you have up to two horsepower at your fingertips, and, little though this amount of power may seem, you must handle it properly or you can get into trouble.

Mopeders come in all sizes, shapes, and ages. If you are, say, thirteen and too young for either a learner's permit or a driver's license, you will have to stay off public thoroughfares in most states. You might, however, have an opportunity to do a bit of off-road riding now and then. Most mopeders range from high-school and college age on through the thirties and forties and well up into senior citizenry.

You don't have to be an athlete or go into any special training to ride a moped. Since the bike has no clutch pedal, gearshift, or footbrake to operate, it is much simpler to ride than a motorcycle. First, however, you should read through the owner's manual so you will have an idea of the key things to look for. Also the dealer should be around to answer any questions that might occur or explain any details that might be slightly confusing.

There are a lot of things you should do before reaching for the engine switch. Adjust the saddle and set the handlebars so that you can easily reach the controls. The saddle should be just high enough so that when you sit squarely on it, your heels rest on the pedals at their lowest position. Use your heels on the lowered pedal strictly as a measuring device. You actually pedal with the balls of your feet, hinging your ankles, or ankling, just as you do when pedaling a bicycle. But because pedaling is only a minor part of moped action, you needn't concentrate on this aspect.

Get in the habit of mounting or dismounting from your bike on the side opposite the muffler. This practice helps keep you from kicking the exhaust pipe or muffler. It also prevents you from burning yourself on the hot metal. However, using the other side is certainly permissable if you find it more natural and comfortable.

With the moped up on its sturdy, center-mount kickstand, climb into the saddle and familiarize yourself with the various controls attached to the handlebars. The first thing you'll note is that, although the grip on the left handlebar tip is solid, the right hand grip turns. As on a motorcycle, the right handgrip is your throttle. Twist inward, or counterclockwise, to speed up the motor. You decelerate, or cut the throttle, by rotating the grip clockwise, in the opposite, or outward, direction. Actually, upon release, the spring-loaded throttle should automatically return to idle position. The throttle should have a positive feel to it, neither loose nor tight, in order to afford sure control.

Now determine that both brake levers are within easy reach of your fingers as your hands rest on the handlebar grips. Squeeze the right lever, which activates the front-wheel brake. Be sure that the cable is taut and responsive to your touch. You don't want much loose play in the lever. If it is too stiff, the brake

52

Both riders keep fingers of left hands ready on the rear brake levers.

shoe may be rubbing the drum when it should not. Check the left lever, which controls the rear brake, in the same fashion.

On the right handlebar, just inboard from the throttle, you will find the off-run switch. It is a simple switch that operates without a key. There may be an extra kill button located adjacent to the switch, by which you can quickly shut off the engine in an emergency. However, in most cases, the easy-to-reach main switch also serves as the kill button.

Now check back on the left side of the handlebar. Beneath the solid handgrip is the starting lever, well below and smaller than the brake lever. Inward on the handlebar you will find the light switch and a horn button. You may even find a choke trigger on the handlebars of some bikes. This control enables you to set the choke without reaching down to the carburetor. However, it is a dubious convenience, since setting a choke is very simple.

You may also find, located elsewhere on the handlebars, a turn-signal switch or paddle, one or more rearview mirrors, and perhaps even the sealed-beam headlight and speedometer, although the latter two usually are mounted on the front forks.

While you're checking the moped, carefully consider the tires. A good practice is to maintain load, speed, and pressure below the maximum stamped on the tires. To exceed any of them is, of course, subjecting yourself to possible trouble. Depending upon the make of tire, its intended use, and so forth, any pres-

54

Checking tire pressure before a ride is a good idea.

sure below the maximum should be sufficient. Most dealers suggest that you carry six to ten pounds more pressure in the rear tire than in the front tire, for example, about 26 psi in the front and 34 psi in the rear.

While the moped is still jacked up on the center stand, check out the wheels to be sure they are not warped or out of line. Sight down each wheel as you spin it. Listen for any gritty or grinding sound. Well-lubricated bearings do not make noises.

Now the time has come to let the dealer start up the motor. Watch the different steps required to do so. If there seems to be an excessive amount of tinkering to get it fired up, ask why. Mopeds are supposed to be simple, uncomplicated machines that start with a minimum of fuss and effort. If the engine balks at starting, make sure you receive a logical explanation.

Have the dealer start the motor more than once. Let it run awhile to warm up. Ask the dealer to shut it off, and kick it over again. Sometimes warm engines are harder to start than cold ones.

Tune your ears to any roughness in the engine. Look and feel for vibrations that are set up when it is running. The engine could be improperly tuned or even insecurely mounted on the frame.

If everything seems all right, if the moped looks, sounds, and feels good to you, take a trial ride. Turn off the motor so you can start from the beginning.

First, of course, make sure you have sufficient fuel in the tank. Mopeds have no easy-to-read fuel gauges. On some you can use a simple dipstick. But most of the time you will need to use the peek-and-shake system. Remove the cap and peer in to catch the liquid reflection of the fuel, or shake the moped and listen for the gurgle. This check is not really critical, for even if you should happen to run out of fuel, you need only reach down and switch the fuel-control valve, or petcock, to the *reserve* setting. This valve sucks extra fuel from a reservoir in the bottom of the tank and puts twenty or so extra miles at your disposal, surely enough to get you to a fuel supply.

You will normally find the petcock at the low end of the tank, just above the carburetor. But not always. (Mopeds are built in factories scattered around the world, so the type, location, and operation of the features on them vary considerably. However, there is a certain standardization, particularly in mopeds sold in the United States, which is helpful.) The standard petcock has three position settings—horizontally forward for *off*, straight down for *on*, and straight up for *reserve*.

Now that you are ready to start the motor, turn the fuel valve so it points to *on*. As the fuel flows into the carburetor, reach to the handlebar and turn the engine switch to run.

If the engine is cold, remember to set the choke. Usually you must reach down to the carburetor and either push or pull a small choke lever. On a few bikes you set the choke through a trigger mounted on the handlebar. If the engine is already warmed up, you can probably forget the choke, depending on the characteristics of the individual machine.

The simplest way to start the engine is to stand beside the machine while it is still up on its kickstand. Bring one of the pedals, either right or left, up a little forward of vertical. If you are right-footed, it may be more convenient to stand on the right side of the machine. Have one hand firmly on the left handlebar grip, with your fingers wrapped around the starter, or decompression, lever. Your right hand should be on the throttle, twisting it counterclockwise slightly off the idle position.

Put your right foot on the upraised pedal, and squeeze the starter lever. Thrust sharply downward on the pedal. A well-tuned machine will kick into action immediately. Release the starter lever right away. Let the machine idle until it warms up a little. Then give the throttle a quick twist counterclockwise to full power. In this way you release the semiautomatic choke. Let the engine warm up a few more seconds,

With moped on its kickstand, start the engine with a downward thrust of the pedal.

and you are ready to go. Do not stand still and keep the engine idling very long, or it probably will overheat. An air-cooled moped engine needs to keep moving in a self-made breeze to maintain a safe, low temperature.

The alternate method of starting the moped is to lower it from its kickstand and climb aboard. Now pedal forward a few revolutions to get up a little momentum, depress the starter lever, and release it as soon as the engine fires up. If the engine doesn't start the first time, resume pedaling and try again. A cold engine may be balky and need extra choking.

Of course, with the engine running smoothly and the automatic transmission sending its energy down the power train to the rear wheel, you can stop pedaling and just cruise along. Most of the time, while cruising, you will find it more comfortable to keep your feet resting on the idle pedals. Bring the pedals up so the cranks are horizontal and the pedals themselves are at approximately the halfway mark. If you bank into a turn with a pedal in full down position, it may catch on the ground and spill you. Some bikes have comfortable footboards mounted above the engine for you to rest your feet on if you wish. However, except on long stretches, you probably will prefer to keep

Keep the pedals at a fairly level position while cruising.

your feet on the pedals, ready to help with a little foot power when needed.

Once the engine is humming along evenly and your speed is up to where you want it, ease the throttle clockwise a quarter turn and reduce power. You won't cut your speed very much, yet you will save fuel and, even more important, there will be less strain on the engine. A tiny moped motor, like any other motor,

61

should not be run at full throttle over long distances or for extended periods of time.

While you are getting accustomed to the machine, toy with the throttle a little. Work it gently through its entire spectrum until you know just what you can expect from the various settings. Familiarity with the throttle is a primary key to pleasant riding.

Another key is the brake system. While riding, your fingers should never stray far from the two brake levers on the ends of the handlebars. Those brakes are your best safety insurance.

In fact, you should keep both hands on the handlebars at most times during a ride. You will, of course, take your left hand briefly off the grip when you make your hand signals to turn or stop. But put it back as quickly as you can.

When the time comes to slow down or stop, squeeze the lever on the left handlebar first. This one activates the rear-wheel brake and starts tugging you to a stop without spoiling the moped's stability. Press the right lever activating the front brake slightly after the rear brake has initiated the slowing action. If you jam the front brake on first, too much weight is thrown forward, which can spoil your steering control and might even send you toppling over the handlebars.

Of course, the action of applying the rear brake first, then adding the substantial stopping power of the front, is basically a continuous motion, with only a slight lag in time from rear action to front action. With a little practice, you will soon be braking to smooth, well-controlled stops automatically.

After you have practiced slowing down normally, you should try a few "panic stops." There may be times when you are riding comfortably along and suddenly a car looms in your path or a child chases a ball into the street in front of you. Then you will have to hit those brakes hard. Even in such an emergency, try to squeeze the left lever for the rear brake a split second ahead of the front. The main thing is to make the tires bite the ground and prevent an accident. If you have developed and practiced your braking habits in the proper way, you will react correctly without thinking.

When you first begin riding, cruise around awhile in an empty parking lot or on an isolated stretch of road. Even a well-packed path will do. Do your practicing where you feel safe. Run through the procedures —starting, accelerating, decelerating, and stopping. With increased skill and confidence comes increased pleasure.

A new rider can use a little support.

When you find a moped that you enjoy riding and decide to buy it, your search is over. Fine. But then you must be willing to abide by the rules and regulations that govern the riding of mopeds.

64

4 Traffic Rules and Regulations

The sudden boom of mopeding in the United States caught many Government agencies unprepared to deal with the newly popularized machines. There were rules for automobiles, motorcycles, motor scooters, and even for bicycles. But a moped was an unknown, unfamiliar vehicle with which to contend. Since it was not a motorcycle, a motor scooter, or a bicycle and it certainly had no real connection with an automobile, special rules needed to be established for its use.

Was it all right to ride a moped on major highways or even on sidewalks? Did it have to be registered and licensed like a motorcycle? Or, like a bicycle, could one simply buy it and use it freely? Should one have a driver's license to operate it? And what about carrying liability insurance in case of an accident? Questions upon questions.

Local agencies weren't sure. State legislators were uncertain. The Federal Government was puzzled.

Mopeds on public streets called for rules and regulations.

Nothing was black or white; the whole subject was shrouded in gray. State laws varied, even when there were laws. Many legislative agencies simply shoved the entire subject of mopeds under the rug. Others gave it halfhearted attention. But by late 1977 there were about a half-million mopeds in the country, and the matter of approving or disapproving their use demanded attention.

66

The states began to deal with mopeds, some in a less than enthusiastic manner. And seldom did one state compare notes on what another was doing. One might restrict the size of the motor to one horsepower, while a neighboring state might conclude that two horsepower was all right. Some states set twenty miles per hour as a maximum moped speed; others permitted twenty-five or thirty miles per hour. In any case, such low speeds were not sufficient to keep up with fast traffic, making it impractical as well as illegal to operate mopeds on interstate and primary highways.

By considering the moped as a motor vehicle, some states decided to require a driver's license to operate one. Other states set a minimum-age limit, usually fifteen or sixteen, which was around the age driving permits were issued anyway. At least, it was widely agreed that a moped is not a toy, that it can be dangerous, that there must be limitations on its use, and that its proper operation requires certain mature judgment. So, through a driver's license or a minimum-age restriction, most states presently screen out those who are too young or inexperienced to be motoring around on public streets.

Another problem was that if a moped was classified as a motorcycle—which it often closely resembles—

it had to be equipped to meet Federal standards, which would, in turn, boost its price and defeat one of its basic purposes: simplicity. Mopeders felt that if they had to meet motorcycle standards, they might as well get a motorcycle.

Advocates of mopeds were fully aware that mopeding had become a basic and successful means of short-range, low-cost transportation all over the world. Millions of people were riding them without numerous rules and restrictions. Although Americans were addicted to high-powered automobiles and high-speed motorcycles that could compete on the interstate highways, there had to be a place for mopeds.

In 1975, an agency called Motorized Bicycle Association was formed. Headquartered in Washington, D.C., its purpose was and is to act as a middleman through which the moped industry could deal with the Government. Its aim is to coordinate ideas, seek some standard of regulation, and promote a better understanding about the safety and the utilization of mopeds.

Even before the MBA, manufacturers tried to get the United States Department of Transportation to classify mopeds in a separate category of vehicles and to establish standards that would be suitable to these lowspeed vehicles.

The separate category was not awarded. However, the National Highway Traffic Safety Administration (NHTSA), an agency of the United States Department of Transportation, did establish a subcategory of motorcycles into which mopeds would fit. The NHTSA called them simply "motor-driven cycles." As long as the cycles abided by the motor limitations of 50cc capacity and 2.0 hp and were geared to speeds not to exceed thirty miles per hour, NHTSA was willing to relax some of the strict standards set up for the larger, more powerful machines.

The adjustments allowed for a smaller stoplight than the one used on motorcycles. They eliminated the requirement for turn-signal lights and modified braking demands and tire requirements. Generally, the moped came to be defined as a lightweight, motor-driven two- or three-wheeled cycle having fully operable pedals capable of propelling the vehicle by foot power if need be. In additon, the moped must have an automatic transmission system, which eliminates foot-clutch pedals and the need for shifting.

The NHTSA also specified that mopeds must have a horn sufficiently loud to be heard for at least 100 feet. The horn button belongs on the left handlebar and is usually combined with the light switch. Also the

Moped Laws—State by State

STATE	CC	POWER	REGISTRATION
ARIZONA	max. 50	1.5 hp or less	yes, $8. yr.
ARKANSAS	max. 50	max. 2 hp	no
CALIFORNIA	none	under 2 gross hp	no
COLORADO	max. 50	max. 2 hp	yes, $5.-3 yrs.
CONNECTICUT	under 50	max. 2 hp	no
DELAWARE	under 50	max. 1.5 hp	yes, $5.-3 yrs.
FLORIDA	none	max. 1.5 hp	no
HAWAII	none	1.5 hp or less	no
ILLINOIS	max. 50	max. 2 hp	yes, $12. yr.
INDIANA	max. 50	max. 1.5 hp	no
IOWA	max. 50	none	yes, $5. yr.
KANSAS	max. 50	max. 1.5 hp	yes, $5. yr.
LOUISIANA	max. 50	max. 1.5 hp	no
MAINE	max. 50	max. 2 hp	yes, $5. yr.
MARYLAND	max. 50	under 1 hp	no
MASSACHUSETTS	max. 50	max. 1.5 hp	yes, $3.-2 yrs.
MICHIGAN	max. 50	max. 1.5 hp	yes, $2 yr.
MINNESOTA	under 50	max. 2 hp	yes, $3 yr.
NEVADA	none	none	no
NEW HAMPSHIRE	max. 50	max. 2 hp	yes, $3. yr.
NEW JERSEY	under 50	max. 1.5 hp	no
NEW MEXICO	under 50	none	no
NEW YORK 1 †	none	none	yes, $5. yr.
2 ‡	none	none	yes, $5. yr.
NORTH CAROLINA	none	under 1 hp	no
OHIO	none	under 1 hp	no
PENNSYLVANIA	max. 50	max. 1.5 hp	yes, $6. yr.
RHODE ISLAND	none	max. 1.5 hp	yes, $10. yr.
SOUTH CAROLINA	none	under 1 hp	no
TENNESSEE	max. 50	max. 1.5 hp	—
TEXAS	under 60	none	yes
VERMONT	50	max. 2 hp	yes, $10. yr.
VIRGINIA	none	under 1 hp	no
WASHINGTON, D.C.	max. 50	max. 1.5 hp	yes, $6. yr.

† *Class-C motorcycle*
‡ *Class-B motorcycle*

70

MAX. SPEED	MINIMUM AGE	LICENSE
25	16	any valid license
30	14	any valid or special license at 14
30	15	any valid license or learner permit
30	16	any valid license
30	16	any valid license
25	16	any valid license
25	15	no
*	15	no
30	16	any valid license
25	15	no
25	14	any valid or motorized-bicycle license at 14; no road test
25	14	any valid license, written test only at 14
25	15	any valid license
30	16	any valid license
*	16	any valid license
25	16	any valid license or learner permit
25	15	any valid or moped license; no road test
30	15	any valid or motorized-bicycle permit
30	16	any valid license
30	16	any valid license
25	15	no
25	*	any valid or restricted license
20	16	any valid or special license
21-30	16	any valid or special license
20	16	no
20	14	any valid or motorized-bicycle license
25	16	any valid license
25	16	any valid license
20	12	no
25	16	any valid license
20	15	written test only
30	16	any valid license
20	16	no
25	16	any valid or motorized-bicycle license; no road test

* *none stated*

```
┌─────────────────────────────────────┐
│           MANUFACTURED BY           │
│       A-1 Motorized Bicycle Co.      │
│            October 1978             │
│                                     │
│             GVWR 425                │
│          GAWR Front 135             │
│             Rear 290                │
│                                     │
│   THIS VEHICLE CONFORMS TO          │
│   ALL APPLICABLE FEDERAL            │
│   MOTOR VEHICLE SAFETY STAN-        │
│   DARDS IN EFFECT ON THE DATE       │
│   OF MANUFACTURE SHOWN              │
│   ABOVE.                            │
│       VEHICLE IDENTIFICATION        │
│          NUMBER 12345               │
│        MOTOR DRIVEN CYCLE           │
└─────────────────────────────────────┘
```

All quality mopeds carry a certification label approved by the Motorized Bicycle Association.

NHTSA encourages plainly labeling important items, such as the off-run switch, the off, on, reserve positions of the fuel-flow valve, and the lights, horn, and choke, to help avoid errors and accidents.

The moped that meets Federal standards carries a certification label permanently fixed on or near the steering post. The label gives the name of the manufacturer, the month and year the machine was made, and the vehicle-identification number. The label also designates the gross-vehicle-weight rating (gvwr) and divides that weight into a gross-axle-weight rating (gawr) for each axle, front and rear. Thus, a moped with a gvwr of 425 pounds may have a gawr of front, 135 and rear, 290. This label serves as a guide to keep the rider from overloading the machine.

The actual serial number of the vehicle will be stamped directly onto the frame, also usually on or adjacent to the steering column. The owner should keep a record of both the identification number and the serial number, and, if one can be found, a motor number. They may come in handy if the bike is stolen.

So now there are standards for mopeds that are approved for use in the United States. Not all machines on the market currently meet these standards, nor is effective policing possible at present. But given time and effort, mopeds will eventually meet Federal standards established to improve their efficiency and safety.

Other regulations, usually state controlled, dictate to a degree where and how you can ride a moped. In essence, you operate a moped under the same rules of the road that apply to any other motor vehicle. You have to cut throttle in school zones or any other areas posted for reduced speeds. You are expected to stop at signs or signals. You ride with the traffic on the right-hand side of the street, you give proper arm signals when needed, you stay off sidewalks, and you use public streets and thoroughfares only if you carry a proper permit or license.

There are attempts under way to pass legislation that will allow a person who is a year or so shy of

Give appropriate traffic hand signals.

being eligible for a driver's license to receive a special permit for mopeding. He or she will probably have to pass a written rules-of-the-road test, have good eyesight, and be sufficiently fit for mopeding, which could require strenuous pedaling at times. Such special licenses for fully qualified young people do seem reasonable in the light of the fact that very young boys and girls are permitted to ride minibikes and lightweight dirt motorcycles on off-road terrain. And mopeds are usually easier and safer to ride.

So there are rules and regulations involved in mopeding. Ask your dealer what restrictions exist in your area so you will not unwittingly break any laws. And check with your local Department of Motor Vehicles or police department concerning the legalities of mopeds in your city or state.

You can get the most fun and use out of your moped by riding it in a safe, legal fashion.

5 A Matter of Safety

You must face the fact that when you are riding a moped you are not the king of the mountain. Nor do you have the ton or more of protective metal around you that an automobile provides. Legally, you enjoy most of the same rights and privileges of other motorists. But your two-horsepower vehicle is surrounded by two-hundred-horsepower vehicles. So you had better mind your manners.

Learn to follow this credo: Pretend you are invisible. Ride as though neither motorists nor pedestrians can see you. Often they don't. Your best bet, therefore, is to keep a sharp eye out for them and anticipate what they might do. Keep a safe distance from everything. Leave yourself a way out in case something happens unexpectedly. Ride defensively, never aggressively.

Machine for machine, mopeders have far fewer accidents than motorcyclists yet more than bicyclists.

The added weight and the engine power are factors you must consider at all times. They can aid your stability and ease the burden of propulsion, but they also can get you into trouble.

One of the most important safety rules in mopeding is to accept the fact that the right-of-way is never yours. Legally it may be, but practically it is not. Sitting astride a 100-pound motorized bicycle is no time to argue rights-of-way with a person coming from the left in a station wagon.

> Remember the story of Mr. Jay
> He died defending his right-of-way.
> He was right—dead right
> As he sped along.
> But he's just as dead now
> As if he'd been dead wrong.
> —Anonymous

The majority of moped accidents, some serious, occur at intersections, when the motorist does not see or hear you approaching on your small vehicle. Some motorists resent mopeders and refuse to recognize their rights. Worse still, a few motorists take delight in crowding mopeds off the road. So you must always

Lightweight bicycle-type helmets are favored by moped riders.

be on the lookout, always ride defensively, always think ahead, and always leave yourself a way out of any unexpected jam.

Even though for safety's sake you may be pretending that you are invisible to motorists and pedestrians, you still should do whatever you can to improve your visibility. Wear bright clothes and a white or colorful helmet. Although you are not always required by law to wear a helmet while mopeding, many riders do. The lightweight bicycle type is most inexpensive and popular, but some use the heavier, more protective motorcyclist helmet. It is a matter of personal selection. In any case, you need goggles or a face shield on your helmet to protect your eyes from wind, dirt, and insects.

Wearing long pants or slacks helps protect your legs from brush scatches, bruises from falls, or burns from the hot exhaust pipe. You should avoid wearing loose, floppy clothing that might catch in the chain or the spokes. An elastic strap or a cyclist's clip placed around the cuffs of pant legs will prevent them from getting tangled. You should also wear laced shoes that will stay on while pedaling.

The fact is, however, that mopeders are seen wearing T-shirts, shorts, and sandals, whether they are tooling around the seashore, driving to the store, or taking a Sunday ride. Indeed, some are even in bathing suits and barefoot. There is no law about what you must wear, but the mopeder should be aware of what he or she is doing and know the risks involved.

One thing to watch out for is riding too close to the center of the road where leaky cars often leave a slippery path of oil and grease. Keep well to the right of the strip but not too close to the curb or in the gutter. When cresting a hill, always stay far to the

Dress to be safe and seen when riding a moped.

right. You never know how much of the road the driver of the vehicle ascending the hill in the opposite direction is taking up. And if it is a truck, you should be as far to the right as you can get.

Trucks or buses of any kind are potential hazards to the mopeder. Whether passing you or coming from the opposite direction, a speeding truck or bus creates a vacuum of air that tends to pull you toward it. They do not suck up mopeds, but the sudden whoosh of air disturbs the balance of lightweight machines. By staying well to the right where you belong, you should have no problem.

You also should avoid mopeding on extremely windy days. Don't worry about a mild breeze, but beware of any wind gusting at more than twenty miles per hour. Not only is the wind apt to upset you if it hits you broadside, the motor may not be able to cope if you head into it. Pedaling will be extremely difficult, and the straining motor is likely to overheat.

It should go without saying that you always ride with the flow of traffic, never against it. Yet at times you will see bicyclists, and even an occasional careless mopeder, disobeying the law by riding on the wrong side of the street. Doing so is extremely dangerous, for the motorist coming toward you may panic at the sight of your machine.

Also, keep your moped off sidewalks. Motorized vehicles of any type are not legal there.

Although your moped has a top speed of somewhere between twenty and thirty miles per hour, you are wise not to try to keep up with traffic. Except in congested areas automobile traffic seldom moves that slowly. Besides, if you are in a real hurry, you probably shouldn't be on a moped.

To insure safe riding, develop the habit of reading the road ahead. Anticipate. Watch out for storm-drain gratings. Beware of large cracks or holes in the pavement. In winter, look way ahead of you for icy patches or rain-slick streets. Sand, spilled gravel, or wet leaves can throw your moped tires into a skid. Ride a straight course. Don't weave and dodge around.

While you are peering ahead and planning your route to avoid hazards—which is what defensive driving is all about—pay particular attention to cars parked along the curb or backing out of a driveway. The door of a curbed car may swing out suddenly, leaving you no alternative but to smash into it or swerve out dangerously into the line of traffic. But if you are moving at a reduced speed and are looking and thinking far enough ahead, you will be able to apply your brakes in time to avoid an accident.

The driver of any car backing out of a driveway or coming out forward, for that matter, may not see you

unexpected hazards for the moped rider

82

on your small moped. The burden is on you to avoid him. Use your horn as soon as you see the car emerging, but apply your brakes quickly too.

If traffic is moving slowly and you are able to keep pace with it comfortably, then move farther out from the curb and occupy your legitimate slot in the right-hand lane. However, you should keep toward the right of your lane and out of the way if traffic speeds up. Leave plenty of room between yourself and both the car ahead and behind, if you can manage it.

Remember that the driver ahead may not be able to see you. You may be riding in his or her blind spot. So be particularly cautious about riding close to rear fenders. Motorists may suddenly turn right and pinch you to the curb or left and make you swerve out. Or they may slam on their brakes. Not only do they have the advantage of acting first and perhaps catching you unprepared, but four-wheeled automobiles can stop in less distance than a two-wheeled moped.

Don't, of course, forget the car behind you. If aware of your low power and vulnerability, the motorist will probably be considerate and stay well back. But keep the car in sight in your rearview mirror anyway, and try to maintain the distance of at least two bike lengths between you. Don't rely entirely on your mirrors to

Leave plenty of room between yourself and surrounding cars.

keep you informed about what is going on behind you. Occasionally pivot your neck and peek quickly over your shoulder to keep everything in proper focus.

At all times, of course, you must use plain, correct traffic signals so everyone around you knows what you intend to do. Even if you have lighted turn signals on your moped, back them up with hand signals. Keep your right hand on the throttle, and point your left hand straight out for a left turn, raise your left arm up from the elbow for a right turn, and lower your left arm at a downward angle to indicate slow or stop. Return your left hand to the handlebar grip as soon as you can. You need both hands for full steering control. And don't forget to keep your left fingers on the brake lever in order to apply the rear brake first when stopping or slowing down.

Be wary of quick, white-knuckle stops that put you into a skid. Jamming on your brakes while making a high-speed turn also invites trouble. Sometimes you

Give early and plain hand signals.

can apply brakes off and on quickly and repeatedly to prevent your tires from losing traction. But the best way to avoid any problem is to slow down and make your turn at a safe speed.

Avoid making left-hand turns whenever possible. Approaching such a turn puts you on the inside lane of the road, where traffic moves the fastest and where you are most vulnerable. Besides, to make a left-hand turn you must cross in front of traffic coming from the opposite direction, which is always risky on a low-powered moped. If you decide to hazard a left-hand turn in traffic, by all means give way to any oncoming vehicles first.

A better procedure is to avoid making the turn altogether. Simply keep to the right of the road, dismount at the intersection, and use the crosswalks. Just be sure to walk your moped when using crosswalks.

When you are riding on secondary roads where traffic is light, there may be less tension per mile, but there still are potential perils to which you must be alert. Don't ride on the shoulders of the road. Some are soft, but others have a tendency to narrow down near culverts, bridges, and hills. Thus, you find yourself suddenly having to swing back onto the main road and into the flow of traffic. Also, shoulders of roads are apt to be sprinkled with rusty nails, broken glass, loose gravel, and other debris, all of which are rough on mopeds. You may even have to climb a sharp lip to get back on the pavement, which is an easy way to flip. Whenever possible, always stay on the main part of the road, where you belong.

Most important, it should go without saying that no mopeder with any regard for safety would try to hitch a ride by grabbing hold of a moving vehicle.

Mopeding is a highly social activity. The more the merrier, as they say. But, with few exceptions, a moped is not built for riding double. Indeed, a few machines sport buddy seats, have extra-sturdy construction, and are equipped with two-speed transmissions. Their makers claim it is safe to ride double on them, which is no doubt true insofar as the machine is concerned. But if you do ride double, you had better be extra skilled and extra careful. Most mopeds are not built for the extra weight and strain that riding double puts on them. The suspension system won't take it, the tires can blow, the seat is crowded, and the small engine will suffer excessive wear trying to haul around added weight.

When several mopeders get together on separate machines both the fun and the hazards multiply.

Riding side by side along the street so you can talk is unsafe when there is traffic to contend with. The mopeder riding on the inside or toward the center of the road is particularly vulnerable to automobiles coming from the opposite direction. You might find yourself in a situation where you can get out of the way only by plowing into the other mopeder next to you. So ride single file, no matter how many others are in your party. Stay a couple of bike lengths behind each

Ride single file for safety.

other, and stagger your positions a little to one side or the other so that the rider ahead does not block your visibility.

There are a few other hazards you may encounter while mopeding. A child suddenly runs out from behind a car. A cat darts across the street. A dog chases you. Suddenly you have to slam on the brakes or dodge out of the way. In the case of a dog, don't try to outrun him or blip your throttle menacingly at him. Pay as little attention to him as possible, and maintain your normal speed. The dog should quickly tire of the game and amble off. However, if it doesn't, you may have to stop and get off your bike. Keep the moped as a barrier between you and the dog until help arrives.

You must keep an eye out for pedestrians and bicyclists. They, like you, are not always plainly visible. Unfortunately, collisions sometimes are causes for lawsuits. For this reason, whether or not your state requires it, consider carrying some kind of insurance to cover mopeding accidents.

There is a great deal to think about in order to ride a moped safely. But the practical utility of the vehicle and the fun gained from mopeding are well worth the attention.

6 Care and Maintenance

A moped appears to be a very simple piece of machinery. Yet, despite the simplicity of a moped's design, there is a large collection of nuts and bolts, chains and gears, tubes and bearings, wheels and pedals, and other paraphernalia that make up the vehicle. All of it takes regular care and requires periodic maintenance if you hope to have it serve you properly.

There are many things that you, as the moped's proud owner, can do to keep it in top condition. There are, however, other things better left to a certified moped mechanic, who may be associated with the dealer from whom you bought your moped. Where your care and maintenance ends and where the dealer's begins depends largely upon how mechanically adept you are.

The owner's manual—and be certain that one comes with your moped—will detail steps you can take toward its care. First, you should keep the machine clean and tight. Plain water and a rag or sponge is as good a way as any to keep the paint and chrome clean. It is best not to use detergents or solvents on your moped unless the vehicle is particularly dirty or greasy. Regular car wax will brighten up paint and put a sheen on stainless-steel fenders. Special cleaners and protectors are available for plastic or chromed parts. There is considerable detail work in cleaning a moped from

Keep your moped clean.

spokes to saddle, but you will be rewarded by its smooth operation and the pride of owning a clean, handsome bike.

Along with the cleaning, you should periodically check and tighten all screws, nuts, and bolts. Engine vibration and the jolting of street riding tend to loosen the machine. Sometimes you get a warning rattle or a squeak, but sometimes you may not be aware of a loose nut or screw until a part falls off.

You will, of course, need a few simple tools. Most mopeds have a small tool kit someplace on the bike. The contents should include appropriate end wrenches, a spark-plug wrench, perhaps a wire brush for cleaning the plug, and a screwdriver or two. A six-inch adjustable wrench also comes in very handy. If you have room and want to go further, carry a spare plug, a light bulb or two, a bit of wire, a small can of oil, several extra chain links, and a cleaning rag. What you can carry along depends upon the racks or containers you may have on your bike. Since most mopeds are foreign made, all measurements are listed in metrics, a system to which the United States is converting. So when buying any special tools you may need for working on your bike, be sure they check out with the manufacturer's specifications.

You must become adept at mixing oil and gas into a proper fuel. For the first 300 or so miles of breaking in a new machine you will use a richer than normal oil-and-gas mix. The additional amount of oil may make your moped smoke a little, but it will provide the lubrication needed to help the moving parts seat

A few basic tools are needed for maintenance.

in properly. During this time keep off the steep hills and don't strain your engine by going over twenty miles per hour.

After the running-in period, begin mixing your fuel according to the specifications in the owner's manual. Since a two-stroke engine does not have a wet crankcase—that is, an oil-filled crankcase—the piston, connecting rod, and crankshaft must get their lubrication from the fuel itself. Thus, a little oil is mixed right into the gasoline, and, although the oil is ignited and burns with the gas, enough gets to the parts to keep them lubricated.

Probably the most common proportion of gas to oil is fifty to one (50:1)or a 2 percent mixture. However, this ratio can vary greatly according to the make of engine and the manufacturer's recommendation. Always mix your fuel exactly according to the owner's manual for your particular machine. Beware of any suggested variations. And be sure they are made by a mechanic who knows your machine and has a valid reason for altering the fuel formula.

All two-stroke moped motors use regular gasoline. There is no advantage in using premium. In fact, it can cause excessive fouling in the motor. Nonleaded gas is worse still.

You must also be particular about the type of oil you use. Special two-cycle oil, SAE 30 or 40, is recommended by manufacturers of two-stroke engines. Not only does it do a good job of lubricating, it is formulated to reduce the buildup of carbon deposits that tend to plague two-cycle engines.

In a pinch, a high-quality, nondetergent car oil (SAE 40–50) can be used in moped fuel mixtures. Make the mix a little richer, say, thirty-five or forty to one, since regular oil doesn't have the high-heat, lubricating qualities of the special oil. Also, by using automotive oil you can expect more carbon or coke to collect in the engine, and you will need to have it decarbonized more often. Since oil is used in such small amounts, use only the best two-cycle oil.

Most mopeders premix their fuel. At fifty to one, the mixture figures out to be slightly more than two and a half ounces of oil to a gallon of regular gas. The gas caps on many moped tanks are designed to serve as measuring cups when they are turned upside down. Normally one capful mixes with one quart of gasoline. If you put four capfuls of oil in a nearly full gallon can of gas and shake it up well, you then have up to 150 miles' worth of fuel to put in your moped tank.

Some mopeders mix their fuel in larger amounts and keep it in a safety container in their garage.

In an emergency, you can add the measured amount of oil directly into the almost full gas tank. Then simply rock the machine vigorously back and forth until you feel it is properly mixed.

At least one manufacturer has a special oil cylinder fastened right onto the machine with a tube leading into the tank. Instead of premixing your fuel, you first put gas in the tank and then unscrew and pull up an activator rod atop the cylinder. Pump it the number of times needed to inject the correctly measured amount of oil into the gas tank. The operation is very convenient. Many other moped manufacturers are working on automated-fuel-mixing devices.

Whatever method you use to fuel your moped, give it particular care and attention. Too lean a mix can cause an engine to seize or burn out. Too rich a mixture causes rough running, misfiring, and quickly cokes up a machine.

Since fuel is your first consideration in getting anywhere on your moped, you should also know how to keep it flowing freely from tank through carburetor and right into the crankcase. If fuel isn't getting through, check and clean the fuel-tank strainer, which usually is part of the fuel valve at the tank. It is not difficult to get at and clean. But, before taking the valve apart, be sure the fuel tank is empty.

Check any other type of filter that might be on the fuel line leading to the carburetor. Different machines have different arrangements.

Most important, examine the carburetor, for most

Cleaning the air filter is a simple task.

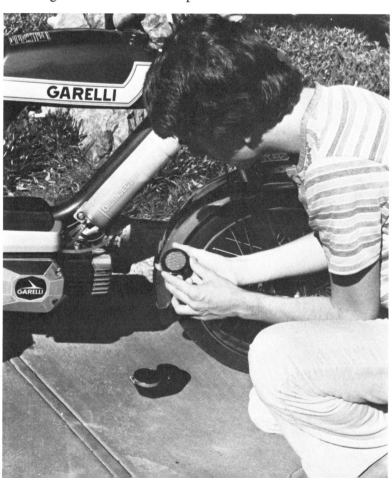

fuel problems center there. Consult your owner's manual to find out how to get to and clean the air filter, usually a simple task. If it is a metallic-screen type, clean and rinse it in solvent or gasoline, dry it well, then coat it with a few drops of light oil before replacing it. If it is a cartridge type, clean it according to instructions or replace it. Replace any filter that is even slightly damaged.

Also check the fuel jet, for a large percentage of fuel-flow problems are caused by a speck of dirt or a piece of lint clogging or partially clogging the jet. Usually you reach the jet by removing the float bowl. Remove the jet and blow it clean. Don't use wire or anything that might scratch the sensitive jet.

Familiarize yourself with the idling screw on the carburetor. Usually it turns clockwise for higher revolutions per minute (rpm's), counterclockwise for lower rpm's. If your moped is set at too fast an idle, it will start to engage your automatic clutch while you are at a standstill. Avoid this danger by setting the carburetor idle screw properly.

If the engine problem isn't associated with fuel, it is likely to be located in the electrical system. The electricity for your moped usually is generated by a flywheel magneto and is one of the assemblies attached to the motor package. A common fault in this system occurs when dirt and debris get into the magneto and foul the contact breaker points. They may become charred, pitted, or get out of adjustment. By consulting your service manual and using a little mechanical know-how, you may be able to get to the contact points and correct the problem. Often there is a window in the flywheel cover for just that purpose. With a fine ignition file or a bit of emery cloth, you may be able to clean the points. Or you may replace them. In either case, you will need to know the proper procedures and have a feeler gauge to set the gap correctly.

Not everyone will be capable of working on the electrical system, however. Most owners probably will be better advised to leave the servicing and correcting of magneto problems to a moped mechanic.

Fortunately, the most common culprit of electrical-system trouble is the spark plug. And correcting is not difficult. The hot running of moped engines rapidly erodes the spark plug's electrode and widens the gap the spark has to jump. In time, the firing becomes erratic, and the clearance must be reset. Usually the proper gap setting is 0.5mm (0.020″). You will again need a feeler gauge to set it just right.

Also, since the oil reaches the combustion chamber along with the gas, the plug is apt to become gummy and fouled. It will need to be washed with gasoline, cleaned with a stiff-wire brush, or sand-blasted fairly frequently. If the porcelain is cracked or the electrodes become worn, replace the spark plug. In fact, since the plug is an inexpensive item, replacing it regularly assures you of a constantly smooth-running, efficient engine.

Check that the ignition wire attaches firmly to the spark plug. Trace all your wiring periodically, testing to make sure that the connections are firm and that the insulation is not becoming worn. Replacing bulbs, when necessary, is a simple task.

You can also clean the chain and adjust its tension. To do a first-class job, open the master link and remove the chain from the bike. Slosh the chain thoroughly in solvent. Use an old toothbrush to clean off any dirt or grease. Dry it as well as you can. Then lubricate it with a good, light, penetrating oil that will put a thin, lasting film of lubricant right into the chain's pins and rollers. Dipping the chain into a warm bath of SAE 90 transmission oil is sometimes recommended. Frequently brushing on a thin outer coat of grease will protect the chain from moisture and rust.

101

A dirty chain wears out quickly, so clean and lubricate it often.

Periodically check the slack in the drive chain. It shouldn't yield more than a half to three-quarters of an inch when you move it up and down with your fingers. Most chains can be adjusted by first loosening the rear-axle nuts. Then, while carefully keeping the wheel centered, use your wrench to turn the drive-wheel-adjustment nuts located on each side of the hub. Don't overtighten the chain, or it will put extra strain on sprockets and bearings. With the chain right and the rear wheel centered, retighten the hub nuts.

Some chains have self-tensioners similar to those on ten-speed bicycles. They eliminate the need for adjusting but certainly not the necessity for periodic cleaning and lubricating.

Some mopeds use V-belts, either instead of or in combination with chains. You adjust this belt in much the same manner that you do a chain, following, of course, the step-by-step instructions given in your manual. V-belts usually require a little tighter tension than chains in order to keep from slipping in their pulleys. About three sixteenths of an inch up-and-down movement is right. Belts don't need lubricants, but they need close watching. If a belt becomes worn and frayed, it is apt to snap and leave you stranded. Try to carry a spare belt if you can.

You also can adjust and lubricate the various levers and cables on your moped. All cables tend to stretch, and control levers develop too much play. A little study will reveal handy adjustment screws and nuts on your bike.

The simplest adjustment is on the far end of the cable. Take it in or let it out to allow about three sixteenths of an inch of free play on the handlebar levers. This setting will assure that the brakes are not dragging with too tight a cable. The clutch cable should be similarly adjusted.

Levers and friction points at either end of each cable should be occasionally lubricated lightly with a drop of oil. To insert lubricant into the cable housing itself may call for a little disassembly near the levers. A squirt or two of light oil, or a special cable lubricant, into the housing will keep the brake, clutch, and speedometer cables operating smoothly. Some cables can be pulled out of their sleeves and lubricated before reinserting. Still other cable shrouds have handy built-in nipples through which you can inject the lubricant.

While you still have the lubricants nearby, once

more check the maintenance schedule in your owner's manual. Inspect your machine with an oil can ready. A drop or two of light oil on the pedals, the suspension springs, the kickstand hinges, and any other exposed points where friction takes place will be beneficial. The secret of good lubricating is to do it consistently—but not overdo it.

The frequency of your visit to a mechanic may be

Remove plug and check level of oil in the gearbox.

measured in time or in mileage, as recommended in your manual. Gearbox and transmission oil has to be changed occasionally. Inevitably dust and grit and water will get into the bearings in the wheels, steering head, and perhaps the pedal cranks. Many crank axles are self-lubricating.

To get to the main bearings to clean, repack, re-assemble, and adjust them usually takes considerable knowledge and skill. Sometimes the work requires special tools. It is not a simple backyard job. Don't be discouraged from trying to do your own service maintenance, however, if you feel qualified. But beware of spring-loaded assemblies that suddenly go twang or ball bearings that start falling out of their races, only to be gobbled up by cracks in the driveway. Before you know it you may be gathering up loose pieces in a box, and taking parts and chassis to your local dealer for fixing up and reassembling. Then you may spend more than if you had gone there in the first place.

When the engine really starts to run roughly, when the clutch begins to slip, when strange chirpings and grindings assail your ears, you may be due for a complete engine overhaul. This point may occur at 5,000, 10,000, 15,000, or 20,000 miles. Some engines can go as far as 25,000 miles between reconditionings. A lot depends on how skillfully you mix your fuel in order to minimize carbon buildup inside the engine and in the exhaust system. If an engine gets badly coked up, it makes possible such unwelcome problems as pre-ignition, overheating, and greater fuel consumption.

A moped should be checked occasionally by a trained mechanic.

Removing carbon from the combustion chamber and piston requires considerable tearing down of the motor and is really shopwork. It can be done most economically in conjunction with other periodic servicing and adjusting.

If you live in cold-weather country and use your moped mostly for recreation, the time will no doubt come every year when you will prefer skiing to trying to maneuver a two-wheeler through deep snow or over icy roads. If you decide to put it in storage until spring, don't just shove it into a corner of the garage and forget it. It will rust, corrode, and gum up, which you should not let happen to a valuable machine.

So clean and dry the vehicle properly before storing it. Spray an anticorrosive oil or a good rust inhibitor on all bright metal parts. Spread a coat of car wax on the painted parts.

Start up the engine, and, while it is running, close the fuel valve, letting it run until the carburetor is empty. Thus, no stale gas and oil will be left to gum up the float and jets. You may want to drain the fuel from the tank also, although doing so is not essential. Remove the spark plug. Inject an ounce or so of anticorrosive oil into the bore. Then pull the starter lever and rotate the engine by moving the pedals to spread the oil over the internal moving surfaces. Replace the plug.

Now you can push the moped into the corner. Put it up on its kickstand to relieve the weight from the tires. Leave the tires inflated. If you throw a cover over the whole machine, you can feel comforted by the fact that, come spring, you will unveil a shiny, unrusted moped, ready to fuel up and ride out into a new season.

So the main advice for keeping your moped in good condition is to do what you are confident of without running the risk of multiplying the complications. What you are not sure you can handle, leave to the experts.

But whichever direction you take—do-it-yourself or have-it-done—the basic truth is that only a well-cared-for and properly maintained machine can provide you with real trouble-free pleasure.

7 Practical and Fun

Mopeds are ridden for two basic reasons—work and fun. Often a moped can fulfill certain transportation needs or furnish a pleasurable ride better than any other means. Thus, the popularity of mopeds is steadily increasing.

Between 1975 and 1977 the annual sales of mopeds in the United States increased sixfold, from about 25,000 units a year to nearly 150,000. At this time, the yearly sales may well have exceeded 500,000, and the goal of selling 1,000,000 mopeds a year will probably be reached soon.

For many years mopeds have been used by workers in other countries to ride to and from their jobs. These employees can operate a moped at minimum cost and without having to expend the physical energy needed for their work.

Now more and more Americans are following their example, using mopeds to go back and forth to their own places of work. In situations where parking space is at a premium, many employers gladly set aside special moped-parking areas. A half dozen or more of the compact vehicles fit easily into the amount of space needed for one family-sized automobile. Parking a moped at home also is a simple matter. With its small wheels and low body, the vehicle takes up less space than most bicycles.

Many small businesses use mopeds for local-delivery service. One delicatessen uses its moped, equipped with wire baskets, to deliver sandwiches and beverages to customers, within minutes after receiving their orders.

Drugstores use mopeds to deliver prescriptions.

Riding a moped to work beats the parking problem.

Auto-supply houses can speed small parts to nearby service stations and other waiting customers. A book dealer delivers the latest best sellers to local shut-ins. A home-style bakery fills the double baskets hung on the back of its moped with fresh breads and pastries for customers.

Actually, as long as the vehicle is not overloaded, an endless variety of items can be delivered by moped. Many establishments that deal in moderate-sized objects have a moped standing by to take on local-delivery service. Often it is the very same one that the proprietor drove to work that morning and the same one that he or she will use for recreation over the weekend.

Messengers, paper boys, and rural mail carriers are turning to mopeds in ever-increasing numbers. The long-familiar tricycle with the big box on the back used by ice cream vendors pedaling through the neighborhood is giving way to three-wheeled, motor-assisted mopeds. Such moped 'trikes,' with extra large baskets or boxes behind the driver and between the rear wheels, also make excellent short-haul delivery vehicles. They are able to carry considerably more than the standard two-wheeled moped.

Trikes are also favored by elderly people for both

recreation and local shopping. They are familiar sights in leisure villages, where many retired people live.

Shopping convenience remains one of the main benefits that mopeders get from their vehicles. When there is a moped handy, the shopper does not need to

Mopeds are very adaptive.

fire up the family car to go for a dozen eggs. The variety of shopping that can be done by moped is virtually limitless.

Regardless of the purpose for which one uses the vehicle, a mopeder should always carry a good locking device. Since mopeds are so new and popular, as well as easy to sell in the next town or county, they are prime targets for thieves.

A moped does not usually have an ignition-switch lock like an automobile. So, unless the machine is properly secured, anyone with know-how can start it up and ride it away. The steering-fork locks built into most mopeds wrack the front wheel sharply to one side, which prevents someone from getting on it and riding it away. However, a moped is light enough so that almost anyone can lift it and put it quickly into a van or pickup truck. When leaving a vehicle unattended, therefore, a mopeder should fasten it to a lamppost, a telephone pole, a tree, or a solidly anchored bicycle rack with a heavy lock and case-hardened chain. A locking gas cap also helps discourage vandalism.

Future moped owners might consider the advantages of these bikes as an excellent low-cost, low-effort vehicle for going back and forth to school. Students by

Mopeds are easily stolen, so lock yours securely.

the thousands, both high school and college, make extensive use of the handy, uncomplicated machines. On many campuses they are replacing bicycles to a large degree.

At school, a moped is used to get from class to class

on time. Some schools are so spread out that students often find it difficult to keep up with their crowded schedule afoot. A moped can make the difference between being on time or being tardy. With parking space at a premium at so many schools, the administration often encourages mopeding by setting up special parking privileges and facilities. Some schools have coin-operated or free, self-locking racks for security purposes. Such arrangements for mopeders have eased automobile congestion on many high-school and college campuses.

Police and security people put mopeds to good use. An officer on a moped seems less threatening than if he were on a motorcycle or in a car. Mopeds are handy vehicles for patrolling parks too. Visitors to New York City's Central Park are familiar with the sight of policemen patrolling the bicycle pathways on their quiet, put-putting two-wheelers. Security patrolmen overseeing large shopping malls also find mopeds an effective way to make rounds and check out their areas of responsibility.

Although mopeds are not designed as dirt bikes, they do have their uses on farms and ranches. The moped can go on any ground that is sufficiently solid, is not overly brush covered, and not too steep. Farmers can ride out across the meadow and bring in the cows. Or they can ride fence with a moped, carrying pliers, cutters, wire stretchers, and repair tools.

Ranchers can check their windmill or water hole. They can ride out to change the irrigation water and

the ideal vacation vehicle

count sheep from the vantage point of the moped seat. All types of chores lend themselves to mopeding.

The other broad use of mopeds can be summed up in one word—*fun*. Mopeds have become a favorite plaything in the United States. There is a generous sprinkling of them just about anywhere that people are having a good time: at lakeshores, beaches, mountains, desert resorts, and other recreational areas.

Much of the pleasure you can look forward to when you own a moped will be in riding around the neighborhood, visiting friends, and enjoying outdoor activities. Mopeding for fun can be a fine social activity. The larger the group of mopeders that get together, the more delightful a two-wheeled safari becomes.

You may want to pack picnic lunches and head out into the country. Those without carrier baskets can lash their boxes and thermos bottles to their rear racks with bungee tie-downs. Someone might pack a portable barbecue and a small bag of charcoal. Such a day can be fun, both on and off the mopeds.

If you decide to buy a moped, you may soon want to range much farther out, amid the sights, sounds, and the fresh air of newly explored country. You might meet a camper on your trip, with a moped racked above the front bumper. The driver is taking a moped

to still more distant parts of the country. Why not? Mopeds are easily transported inside of vans or station wagons or pickup trucks. Bumper racks also are available for carrying a moped on a car.

So, given such portability, you can anticipate the thrill of widening your future areas of exploration and fun. When doing so, make careful plans. Don't look for just any trail. The trail should be reasonably level, smooth, hard-packed for best maneuverability.

But just as important, the trail has to be approved for mopeding. Some state and national parks and recreation areas have such trails; some do not. Some forest lands accept mopeds, provided they are equipped with proper mufflers to control sound and sparks. Before taking to a trail, check whether permission is needed and what the restrictions are.

Also remember that you should stick fairly close to civilization, particularly if you are riding alone. It is both awkward and inconvenient to have a mechanical breakdown or run out of fuel along some distant and isolated trail. At best, you will have to pedal the vehicle back, and dead-engined mopeds do not pedal

a collapsible moped

easily. At worst, you will have to walk the bike home or leave it and go for help. Mopeds are not intended for serious off-road exploring.

But the things that can be done with a moped are nearly as broad as the horizons of one's imagination. Mopeding is practical. It is adventuresome. It is, above all, fun.

Glossary

Buddy seat—a long seat, or saddle, on which two can ride.

Cable—wire or coil spring running through a flexible housing to operate the brake, throttle, speedometer, starter lever, etc.

Carburetor—the mechanism for mixing fuel and air to be injected into the engine.

Choke—device that feeds extra fuel into carburetor for starting a cold motor.

Clutch—friction device for engaging engine to drive chain.

Crank—forged rod to which a pedal is attached.

Cubic centimeter—cc, 0.016 cubic inch. Used in measuring cylinder volume.

Cylinder capacity—*see* Displacement.

Decarbonize—remove unwanted residue of carbon that collects inside of an engine.

Decoke—*see* Decarbonize.

Displacement—volume of cc's inside of the cylinder, cylinder capacity.

121

Drive chain—main chain or belt carrying power from the engine to the back wheel.

Filter—attachment for cleaning air or fuel before either go into the carburetor.

Front fork—twin prongs, often including shock absorbers, between which the front wheel fits.

Handlebar stem—piece that fits into headset and holds the handlebars.

Headset—upper forward part of frame into which handlebars fit.

Jet—small calibrated hole through which fuel is fed into carburetor.

Kickstand—a hinged center stand that supports the moped upright.

Lean fuel—relative to mopeds, gasoline having lesser amounts of oil mixed with it.

Magneto—electricity-generating mechanism run off the engine.

Mag wheel—a wide wheel in which rim and spokes are cast in a single unit.

MBA—Motorized Bicycle Association, a cooperative agency made up of moped manufacturers and distributors.

Moped—a motorized, pedal-assisted vehicle.

Mpg—miles per gallon.

Motorized bicycle—general category of vehicles into which a moped fits, although a slight misnomer, since few even remotely resemble bicycles.

Muffler—engine-exhaust quieting device.

Pannier—saddle bag designed for mopeds or motorcycles.

Petcock—valve that controls fuel flow from the gas tank.

Pod—special carrying basket for mopeds or lightweight motorcycles.

Rich fuel—moped gasoline containing more than normal amount of oil.

Rpm—revolutions per minute that an engine rotates.

Saddle—seat.

Seat tube—upper rear upright of frame into which the saddle post fits.

Spark plug—part fitted into the cylinder head to generate a spark to ignite the fuel mixture.

Starting lever—lever on the handlebar used to engage the engine.

Step-through frame—open frame with no high, horizontal bar.

Suspension—shock-absorber mechanism designed to ease the ride.

Throttle—right-hand twist grip on handlebar that controls the engine speed.

122

Transmission—usually a series of gears that transmits engine power to the wheels.

Two-stroke—a two-cycle engine with one complete up-and-down revolution of the piston with each firing of the spark plug.

Wheelbase—distance between points where front and rear wheels touch the ground.

Index

124

About the Author

Charles (Chick) Coombs graduated from the University of California at Los Angeles and decided at once to make writing his career. While working at a variety of jobs, he labored at his typewriter early in the morning and late at night. An athlete at school and college, Mr. Coombs began by writing sports fiction. He soon broadened his interests, writing adventure and mystery stories, and factual articles as well. When he had sold over a hundred stories, he decided to try one year of full-time writing, chiefly for young people, and the results justified the decision.

Eventually he turned to writing books. To date he has published more than sixty books, both fiction and nonfiction, covering a wide range of subjects, from aviation and space, to oceanography, drag racing, motorcycling, and many others. He is also author of the Be a Winner series of books explaining how various sports are played and how to succeed in them.

Mr. Coombs and his wife Eleanor live in Westlake Village, near Los Angeles.